Living
Our Dream:

A Window Into The Cloister

Sister Mary Gemma Robinson

(Holy Spirit Adoration Sister)

TABLE OF CONTENTS

Prologue

Where there is life there are dreams and dreamers. A person without a dream is like a ship that drifts aimlessly on the sea of life without a compass to guide it. This story is based on the dream of one man, Father Arnold Janssen. Father Arnold was a man of vision who saw the spiritual and material needs of humanity especially in third world countries and had the determination and courage to make his dream of helping all peoples a reality. He envisioned a missionary community of religious men and women who would spread the good news of Jesus Christ at home and abroad, and would help alleviate the sufferings of peoples everywhere. As a result he founded the missionary Society of the Divine Word in 1875 and the Holy Spirit Missionary Sisters in 1889.

From the very beginning Arnold Janssen's dream included a community of cloistered Sisters devoted to perpetual adoration of the Blessed Sacrament who, through their lives of total dedication, would obtain God's blessing on the human race and hasten the spread of his kingdom on earth. This was realized in 1896 when Father Arnold established the Holy Spirit Adoration Sisters with the help of Adolfine Toennies, a school teacher who left books and classroom behind to follow her dream of a life totally committed to God and all peoples. As co-foundress of this cloistered-contemplative community, Miss Toennies, later known as Mother Mary Michael, became the first superior general and lovingly guided the Congregation during the first thirty-seven years of its existence. That God's blessing was with this new community was evident in the influx of young women who were attracted to this way of life and joined the little group of pioneer Sisters in their convent in Steyl, Holland.

Mother Mary Michael was a woman fully alive with good common sense and a great desire to establish as many chapels of perpetual adoration as possible, even in remote mission districts, where her spiritual daughters would love and adore Jesus Christ on behalf of all. At the time of her death in 1934 she had the joy and satisfaction of having made eight foundations of her community in various parts of the globe: Holland, Germany, the United States, the Philippines and China. Today the number of foundations of the Congregation has doubled, with convents in Argentina, India, Brazil and Poland.

Father Arnold Janssen and Mother Mary Michael were people who saw the designs of God in their dreams and, in spite of their own human weaknesses and the difficulties they would encounter, made their dream come true.

On October 19, 1975 the Catholic Church gave official recognition to the sanctity of Father Arnold Janssen when Pope Paul VI beatified him along with Father Joseph Freinademetz, one of his first missionary priests to work and labor for Christ's kingdom in China.

As a member of the Congregation of the Holy Spirit Adoration Sisters, I wish to share our lives and dreams, and lift the veil of mystery which sometimes seems to envelop religious living a cloistered life.

The dreams recorded in the chapters ahead are the dreams of living and deceased women who have lived a cloistered-contemplative life of prayer, especially through the Eucharist, the Liturgy of the Hours and adoration.

The stories related are true, but names have been changed for the purpose of this book.

1. The Pilgrimage

"God, through his Spirit, who is Love, has called us and gathered us together into a religious community whose members are entirely dedicated to the contemplative life and the service of perpetual adoration and thus serve the Church's missionary activity."
　　　　　　　 – Rule of the Holy Spirit Adoration Sisters

At the moment of birth our pilgrimage of life begins. There are a variety of routes we can choose during this pilgrimage, each of which can lead us to our destination of everlasting happiness and possession of God. As our ancestors in faith wandered through the desert in search of the promised land, so we journey through life in search of that peace and happiness for which we were created and which can be found in God alone. After years of restless wandering and sinful self-indulgence, St. Augustine finally realized the purpose of life when he stated, "Our hearts are created for you, O God, and they are restless until they rest in you."

There are many similarities between our earthly pilgrimage and the pilgrimage of God's chosen people through the desert. Each day brings new choices to be made, choices which influence and determine the course of our journey. In reading the Book of Exodus we discover that the Jewish people made some poor choices, and even sinful ones, which estranged them from God so that there were times when they no longer experienced His guidance and protection. This prolonged the time of their exile and suffering, and they wandered aimlessly in the desert in search of the land "flowing with milk and honey."

One unhappy choice that people in every generation make is to close their ears to the voice of God within them. We are afraid to listen for fear that God might ask more than we care to give or that we will have to sacrifice pleasures which we enjoy. As a result we lose ourselves in continual noise and activity so that we do not have to face the desolation within us caused by the absence of God's word. And yet it is only in listening to the word of God and responding to it that we can find the peace, happiness and fulfillment for which we are searching.

As Holy Spirit Adoration Sisters we have followed the same route in our pilgrimage. We keenly realize that God has brought us together to form a community of love with His own love as the basis and foundation. This love we endeavor to share not only with one another but with all peoples by means of the contemplative life and the service of perpetual adoration. As the commentary on our Rule states: "By our way of life we are to witness to the basic truth that God is the true center of being and the goal of history, that He alone can satisfy the human heart, and that every good and every success on this earth are his free gifts."

God is a God of mystery. Through the Prophet Isaiah he said, "So are my ways higher than your ways, and my thoughts than your thoughts." Our vocation is a mystery even to us, but with faith and confidence each of us set out on our journey into the unknown as we embraced a cloistered-contemplative life as Holy Spirit Adoration Sisters in search of the fulfillment of our dream. Although we share the same dream, how different we are in personality, nationality, education and background! From the pilgrimage of life, God can and does call the most unlikely of people to follow the same route or, rather, he inspires in their hearts the same dream.

Since ours is an international Congregation with foundations on four continents, in some of our convents you will find Sisters of as many as seven nationalities. It is an educational and enriching experience to share life so intimately with other like-minded women from a variety of cultures, each of which complements the others and has its own special charism to offer towards the wholeness of the community.

In my experience, the difficulties that sometimes arise because of culture clashes are minimal compared to the benefits reaped, and are mostly due to a lack of knowledge and understanding. To illustrate this last point, our Sisters from tropical climates have the knack of always walking leisurely and working calmly (a great asset for contemplative life!) in contrast to the American and European Sisters who tend to be quicker and in a hurry. During an eight-week stay in our convents in the Philippines, where I had been sent by our superior general to attend a course on religious formation held in one of our convents, I experienced myself that in order to survive the hot climate it was necessary to do everything calmly and leisurely. Never before did I walk so slowly through corridors and up and down stairways. It made me realize that our Filipina Sisters stationed abroad in countries that have the four seasons could be misunderstood by those who have never experienced living in the tropics.

Each Sister has her own unique background and a story could be told of each. Some of our Sisters were professionals before their entrance - nurses, teachers, dentists, musicians - while others came directly from school or an office job. Some were raised on farms and now beautify our cloister gardens with their natural talent to make even the most scrawny of plants healthy and beautiful. All of us, no matter what our background and education, were drawn together along the pilgrimage of life by a power greater than ourselves. The Holy Spirit, by a diversity of ways which is evident in each Sister's own unique story of her vocation, has invited us to dwell in the shadow of his wings.

How true it is that God loves variety, and it is from a variety of backgrounds he draws us. Our Sister from Iowa was a registered nurse following a promising career in the U.S. Navy when at age thirty-two she decided to change careers in favor of helping others by a life of prayer and sacrifice. At the same time her medical expertise was put to good use in caring for the health of our Sisters. In contrast to age and experience, Postulant Jennifer, who left parents and six younger brothers and sisters at the early age of nineteen, was overcome by homesickness those first weeks in the cloister. Each evening would find her sitting on the main stairway crying. When compassionate Sisters would bend over to console her, they always got the same sad cry, "I miss the kids!" Postulant Jennifer knew what she wanted, though, and persevered to follow her dream.

Sister Mary Samuele and Sister Ann Marie came from different religious backgrounds. The former was a Jewess who converted to Catholicism amid much protest from her family and the latter a former Methodist who embraced Catholicism at age seventeen. When Sister Mary Samuele embraced religious life, members of her family disowned her, but the power of her dream was greater than the bonds of flesh and blood. Sister was proud of her Jewish heritage and often remarked that she had the fullness of faith: from Judaism to Christianity to a consecrated life in religion. No one ever read passages from the Old Testament with such enthusiasm and expression as Sister Mary Samuele. Each year during the liturgical cycle, the community would eagerly look forward to her plaintive rendition of King David's cry over the death of his son, Absalom. It was a spine-tingling experience that made an impression lasting through the hours of the day.

Our backgrounds and personalities may differ, but faith is the one common prerequisite we must all possess. Without faith our way of life is meaningless. We seldom see the results of our lives of prayer and sacrifice but we believe in the infinite goodness of God who assures us that he hears every prayer and opens the door to those who knock. (cf Mt 7:8)

Faith keeps us united as a vibrant community on the way to our common goal, just as it was a unifying force that made the chosen people of God one in mind and heart during their exodus through the wilderness in search of the land God had promised them. There were times when the faith of this people grew weak and they complained and murmured against God and their leaders, to their own detriment. We, too, are aware that when there is insufficient faith in our way of life, a person's entire system of values is distorted. Then self-denial, in the many and various forms it takes, becomes extremely difficult.

When a person reaches a decision to embrace religious life it is faith that gives the strength and courage needed to leave family and home, and to sacrifice possessions. We leave the physical presence of family and friends only to find them again in the deeper level of spiritual giving and union which, in Christ, transcends time and distance.

It took great faith on the part of Sisters who had to leave home secretly due to parental opposition to enter our community. Some of the stories border on the dramatic and take us back in spirit to the days of St. Clare of Assisi and St. Thomas Aquinas, both of whom had the same experience. The parents of one Sister sent the police to the convent to persuade her to return home, but there was nothing the police could do since Sister was a willing "hostage." The father of another Sister said he would shoot her if she entered the cloister. Sister knew the threat was made by a distraught father who deeply loved her but, nevertheless, she decided not to take any chances! For weeks after her entrance she knelt in the cloister organ loft during times of prayer, unseen by anyone in the visitors' chapel.

Happily, with time and prayer, in these and all such cases the families eventually become reconciled to their daughters' decision and were even happy and proud about it. It is strangely true that in most cases in which parents were opposed to their daughter's vocation, they eventually became good friends and benefactors of the community. I enjoy thinking of this as a reward from God for the faith and trust these Sisters had in him; a faith that believes everything works together for the good of those who love him.

But it is the daily living of our vocation which challenges our faith the most and demands at every moment a whole-hearted "yes" to the One who has called us and continues to nurture and sustain us with his grace. Our Co-foundress, Mother Mary Michael, said, "As in nature, so in human life, there is light and darkness, sunshine and rain, warmth and cold. Everything should praise the Lord." This is as true in religious life as it is in every other vocation, and yet this rhythm of emotional ups and downs, the contrast of the pleasant and unpleasant, the fervor and the dryness, can test our efforts to live on a faith level, and in the process, enable us to grow in trust as we interpret every aspect of life through the eyes of God's leading Spirit.

We experience this in the routine things of everyday life, such as, arising from the night's rest. How ideal if we all awoke in the morning bursting with energy to get to the chapel and begin the day singing the praises of the Lord! But most of us struggle like everyone else to get on our feet with, I might add, the help of a cup of coffee. We also experience this in our daily work which in itself could seem humdrum and unproductive. Faith tells us, however, it is not in doing that our personal value lies but in being. It is our attitude to the work and our intention in performing it to the best of our ability that make it fruitful for God and others. This, too, is the case with our prayer life. Daily we are asked by phone and mail to pray for innumerable intentions. Herein is the intercessory character of our contemplative life, but it is not expressed primarily by articulating these petitions to God but in our being one with Christ in his spirit of love and surrender to the Father.

Perhaps the biggest challenge to our faith is ourselves. As our pilgrimage in religious life progresses and the years pass by, we gain better insight into ourselves. We become increasingly aware of the seemingly dormant shadow-side of our personalities and the brokenness of our lives. There is no immediate solution to this quandary but to strive to be children of light, and in that light to recognize, acknowledge and embrace our inner poverty. Only the light of faith can enable us to do this; faith in the One who made a lasting covenant with us through baptism and religious profession, the One who can transform shadows into light, brokenness into wholeness, and emptiness into fullness. So, in faith we rejoice that God's love and mercy is made manifest in us everyday and, with Mother Mary Michael, agree that "everything should praise the Lord."

The topic of faith in religious life would be incomplete without mention of the simple, childlike faith that Sisters who are longer in religious life have the unique knack of developing. On one occasion our Sister-laundress was observing the maintenance man feverishly and unsuccessfully working to remove a motor from an automatic washer. Quietly and unassumingly Sister got a bottle of holy water and sprinkled the motor. Immediately it was released. The maintenance man was completely bewildered and exclaimed, "That's downright spooky!" But for Sister-laundress it was nothing exceptional. She had great faith in the power of holy water and expected the impossible. Another time our Sister-cook was out of oranges to serve the community. She took the one remaining orange and placed it in front of the statue of St. Joseph in the kitchen, confident that good St. Joseph would provide. He did provide but in an unexpected way.

No oranges were received but a total of twenty-one water-melons were delivered throughout the day from different friends of the convent. Sister hurriedly took the orange away from St. Joseph for fear that more watermelons would arrive. Her explanation of the mix-up was, "St. Joseph must not know the difference between oranges and watermelons." These simple stories illustrate a profound reality: in our journey towards God, faith lightens our way and beckons us onward. In times of suffering it embraces and carries us, giving us strength to endure and, eventually, bringing us to share in the victory of the Risen Christ.

2. Vocation: The Call

"Next to our Faith, we esteem nothing so highly as the gift of our contemplative-missionary vocation, in which we recognize an unmistakable sign of divine love."
— Rule of the Holy Spirit Adoration Sisters

After many years of interviewing candidates for religious life, I think the question most frequently asked is, "Sister, how did you know you had a vocation?" In reality what the questioner wants to know is how she can learn from another's experiences the signs of a true vocation within herself. There are as many different stories of religious vocations as there are persons consecrated by religious vows, but the one common factor that is peculiar to all religious vocations is an inner urge which seems to draw the individual towards a particular form of religious life. This does not necessarily mean that everyone with a religious vocation is spared the pain of leaving things she loves in order to embrace this way of life, but the interior impulse, which is nothing less than God's call, is there creating its own atmosphere of restlessness until it is responded to. Some of the Sisters in my community have told how they tried to resist when they first became aware of this vocation. After years in religious life, they now find it amusing that, like the prophet Jonah, they thought they could run away from the Lord. One Sister took a job with the government to work abroad in Europe for a year, hoping that this drastic change in lifestyle would deafen the inner call that was making itself more and more heard. But God won out, and Sister returned to the U.S. to begin the work of applying for entrance into our Congregation.

Then there was our novice directress who told her novices one day in recreation how she delayed her entrance for a couple of years because she loved nature and dreaded the thought of having to sacrifice her weekly walk through the woods. The novices, who naively considered their directress ready for canonization, were at first somewhat shocked at such a revelation of human weakness, but afterwards found great consolation in the knowledge that even the saints were not confirmed in holiness from the crib but that they, too, found certain renunciations difficult. However, the secret of their success was in making these difficulties stepping-stones to sanctity.

The call of God is always present in one's life, but where and when it is heard differs with each individual. Some hear it in childhood and, although they get side-tracked at times with other interests, they always seem to be heading in the direction of the monastery. This does not mean that these individuals are souls of special predilection or the like. In many instances their motivation for entering religious life can be less than perfect, but God uses all means, the perfect as well as the imperfect, to accomplish his designs. My own experience can be used as an example. When I was six years old my father died after a very brief illness. The reality of death and the sorrow of physical separation affected me deeply. I distinctly remember thinking to myself that I would never marry because of the grief and sorrow I would experience if my husband preceded me in death. This was hardly a pure motive for entering religious life, but I believe God used this experience and motivation to awaken in me the first stirrings of a religious vocation. Several years later there was a feature story about a cloistered-contemplative

Order in the daily newspaper and I was fascinated as I read about these religious who lived totally for God in prayer, solitude and penance. I felt myself drawn and attracted to this lifestyle. As the years passed I went through all the normal stages of young womanhood and at times seriously considered marriage and various forms of religious life. But deep within there was always that attraction and pull towards dedicating myself to God in a contemplative form of life.

Others do not perceive the call of God until they are more settled in life and, in some cases, have even pursued a profession. One of our novices had the unique experience of having others tell her that she had a vocation. Novice Kathleen had considered religious life on and off since her days in grammar school, but the joys of a happy family life and contentment with her job as a medical secretary kept pushing the attraction of religious life aside. It happened that her parish church had a "vocation-fest": a weekend devoted to promoting vocations to the priesthood and Sisterhood. Many of the religious communities in the Archdiocese of St. Louis were represented by displays and literature. The pastor had slips of paper put in the church pews weeks beforehand for the parishioners to write the names of young men and women in the parish whom they thought might possibly have a priestly or religious vocation. Six people wrote our novice's name, including the pastor. Making her way to the parish's vocational exhibition, she gathered all the literature she could find on various cloistered communities, including the Holy Spirit Adoration Sisters. After reading all the brochures, she contacted our convent in St. Louis and began a series of visits which resulted in her entrance the following year.

When God gives the grace of a religious vocation, he likewise endows the person with all the gifts needed spiritually, physically and psychologically to fulfill the obligations of his call. A person may think she is inadequate for such a lifestyle, but it is then that trust in God must come to the forefront in the realization that, like St. Paul, "There is nothing I cannot master with the help of the One who gives me strength." (Ph 4:13) God's graces, His tenderness and compassion can never be overestimated. Pope John Paul II told a group of religious in his pastoral visit to Portugal, " . . . He (God), on his part, is faithful; the graces necessary for perseverance and a happy response to your vocation will never be lacking."

One of the great examples in salvation history of fidelity to the call of God is that of the patriarch Abraham. Abraham's response to that call demanded great renunciation and detachment; Yahweh said to Abraham, "Leave your country, your family, and your father's house for the land I will show you." (Gn 12:1) The promise God made to Abraham, that he would make of him a great nation and that his descendants would be as numerous as the stars of heaven, always demanded an unconditional faith. Abraham's call and God's covenant with him became a source of universal blessing which extends to all ages and to all peoples.

How inestimable the value of one vocation and the faithful response of the one called! God's ways do not change, and he has continued through the ages to demand faith of those he calls. I remember when I was in the process of discerning my vocation, how I wanted some sensible assurance that I had a vocation before I made the final decision to enter religious life. How I wished that God wrote letters! How I wished for some type of visible response from God in regard to his will for me! And all the time God was telling me what he wanted me to do but, in my anxiety, I was failing to listen to him speak to me in the depth of my being. He wanted me to take the step in faith, but I was looking for some certainty before making such a momentous change.

Perceiving whether one has a religious vocation or not is one thing, and deciding which religious community to join is another. The latter could be referred to as a vocation within a vocation. In most cases, it is easy to ascertain whether one is drawn more to a religious community with apostolic works or to a cloistered-contemplative community; whether one is more inclined to be a religious teacher, nurse, social, worker, or to live a hidden life of deep and constant prayer. When a person makes the choice of a contemplative community, there is the further decision as to which contemplative community to choose. Even though all are devoted to a life of prayer and solitude, each differs in spirit and observance. Some of our Sisters found out about the Holy Spirit Adoration Sisters through vocational ads, personal acquaintance with one of our convents or through hearsay. Gods works in a variety of ways.

My own experience in this regard was rather unusual. I had lived most of my life in the neighborhood of my community's Mount Grace Convent in St. Louis, Missouri, but when I began to seriously consider a vocation to the contemplative life, the thought of joining the Holy Spirit Adoration Sisters never entered my mind. It seems to me that the reason for this is that I had the erroneous impression that the "Pink Sisters" (the name by which many people call our community because of the rose color of our habit) were more for young women who were socialites and came from well-to-do families. Whatever gave me this impression I do not know, but it was there and the Lord knew it. When I was in my junior year at high school, I returned home from school one day to begin the task of making a fire in the furnace. As I scooped up a shovel of coal, I thought to myself, "What cloistered Order should I enter?" Very clearly and distinctly I heard the words in my mind, "The Pink Sisters." I was shocked. I stood immobile with the shovel of coal in my hands and thought, "The Pink Sisters! I never thought of them before." A peace came over me as if the search were ended, and the more I thought of the "Pink Sisters" as time passed by, the more I began to feel myself being drawn to the community and its spirituality at Mount Grace Convent.

In responding to a religious vocation, one can encounter a variety of obstacles which, when accepted as a challenge, can be a means of growth. What are some of these obstacles? One of the most common is a lack of courage. We all admire courageous persons, especially when they openly manifest their beliefs in something that is little understood and even ridiculed by others. This type of courage is often called for when a young woman has made the decision to embrace religious life in a cloistered-contemplative community. Some will think she is doing the greatest thing possible, while others will try to convince her that she is "throwing away" her life. It takes courage to surmount any criticism. In addition, it takes a deeply rooted courage to give up possessions, a satisfying career and one's independence and, most of all, the companionship of family and friends. Of ourselves we would never be able to make these sacrifices, but God always endows us with everything we need to accomplish what he asks of us. With our eyes fixed on him we recall the words of Psalm 31, "Be strong, be courageous, all you that hope in the Lord."

A vocation to cloistered life can likewise be stifled by a false concept of freedom. Some people identify the enclosure with a loss of freedom, but it is a mistake to regard freedom merely as an absence of exterior restrictions while ignoring the primacy of inner freedom. Freedom is more than being physically restricted through rules and cloistered walls. In fact, it is paradoxical that these disciplinary measures which cultivate growth in self-knowledge are conducive to inner freedom. When considering such a vocation, a young woman should rather reflect if she has the necessary stamina to limit contacts with the outside world so that through constant prayer and ready penance she may give herself to God alone. (cf PC, 7)* It is the restriction of these contacts which is often mistaken for a loss of freedom. At one time a newly arrived postulant soon discovered that she unduly missed the contacts and activities she had enjoyed before her entrance. Whenever possible she would hang out the window of her room to watch the traffic in the street below. Eventually she asked to be permitted to sit by the cloister door in order to watch the people come to and fro either on business or to solicit the prayers of the Sisters. It was not too long a time before Postulant Susan was on a return trip home with our blessing!

---

*PC-Perfectae Caritatis: Document on the Appropriate Renewal of the Religious Life from Vatican Council II.

Another obstacle is selfishness which makes us cling to whatever enhances our ego, be it possessions, persons or honors. Someone who tends to be selfish will naturally shy away from a lifestyle that is totally geared to sacrificing self for the sake of the Kingdom. In our modern age when people are inundated with a consumer mentality and enjoy so much independence, it is a great challenge to take to heart the words of Jesus, "Sell all that you possess. . . , and, come, follow me." But love makes all things possible.

In the preceding chapter I touched on parental objection. However, in mentioning obstacles to a religious vocation, this point can be touched on again as it is a prominent one. Perhaps this difficulty causes the most suffering because it so intrinsically involves the emotions. While selfishness can hinder the candidate to religious life, selfishness on the part of the parents can also be the cause of parental objection. To list all the reasons for parental objection would be almost impossible since situations differ. Incidents of Sisters who surmounted this difficulty and entered our Congregation are many and varied. We can only admire the faith, courage and love of God that animated them.

Last but not least among the threats to a religious vocation is the inability to make a decision. By this I do not refer to a basically indecisive personality but to a rather normal fear of making a mistake, of doing the wrong thing. "If I could only be sure that this is the right thing to do," are the wistful words that often express this apprehensive attitude. Every new beginning brings with it a host of unanswerable questions: What will the life be like? Will I be happy? Can I persevere? Frequently, therefore, the inability to take the final step is due to the difficulty of letting go of the security of the present for the uncertainty of the future. Willingness to take the risk involves a combination of courage, love, freedom and light-heartedness that will be given to everyone who takes the step of complete faith in God's gentle call. It is a case of living by the truth in order to come to the light, as Christ has said. (cf Jn 3:21)

A Sister of our community, who recently had an anniversary commemorating forty years of religious profession of vows, good-naturedly recalls her indecisiveness regarding her vocation. Several times she postponed the date of her entrance until finally she received a letter from the superior of our community informing her that she was being given one last opportunity to enter and it had to be during the month of June. Our Sister answered the superior that she would enter on June 31! She was quickly reminded that there are only thirty days in the month of June. This "push" was just what she needed to take the final step and enter our community a few days before the deadline.

Fidelity in following a vocation was exemplified in our founding Sisters. Our Congregation began with a small nucleus of women in Steyl, Holland in 1896. Its continuous growth, which now includes eighteen chapels of perpetual adoration in eight different countries, is attributed largely to the faith and generosity of those first Sisters who responded to God's call with a spirit of total self-giving. Within the call of their religious vocation was a further call to leave their homeland to help establish sanctuaries of perpetual adoration throughout the world. Our Convent of Divine Love in Philadelphia, Pennsylvania was the first foundation from our motherhouse in Holland. In 1915 Archbishop Edmund Prendergast, requested Mother Mary Michael to send a group of Sisters to staff the chapel of perpetual adoration he had built in his Archdiocese of Philadelphia. After this initial foundation, other soon followed in various countries, including three more in the U.S.: St. Louis, Mo, Corpus Christi, Tx, and Lincoln, Ne. Many were the sacrifices our founding Sisters had to make in acclimating themselves to different cultures, climates and language. But those of us who now reap the fruit of their labors bless them for their generous response and total commitment to God's call. Pope John Paul II reiterated the Church's esteem and approval of the contemplative life when he said, "Sisters of the contem-plative life! May your vocation be dear to you; it is more precious than ever in today's world, which seems unable to find peace. The Pope and the Church need you; Christians count on your fidelity." (May 13, 1983)

It cannot be sufficiently stressed that the call to reli-gious life comes from Christ. He is bigger than all the diffi-culties that could possible present themselves, and his grace and love are never wanting. A young woman may be absorbed with what **she** is going to do with her life and, in the process, many "voices" are making them-selves heard, both in and around her. Hopefully above this din she will hear and listen to Christ's "unmistakable, gentle and persuasive voice saying, 'Come, follow me.'" (John Paul II)

3. Day by Day

*"Harmonious communal living and the efficient accom-
plishment of our duties require a regular schedule, which
prescribes the times for prayer and work, for silence and
recreation, and for all community gatherings. Fidelity to
this schedule requires selflessness and is an expression of
our love, shown by our considerateness for one another's
time of prayer, work or rest."*

                     – Rule of the Holy Spirit Adoration Sisters

"Sister, what do you do all day?" This is a question I
am occasionally asked by visitors as if it were difficult for
them to imagine what a cloistered Sister would do all day
besides pray. Some months after my entrance into religious life, when homesickness had run its course and I
had finally become very much involved in the community's apostolate, I began to realize what a gift time is and
that there never seems to be enough of it as day follows
day in a flow of prayer and work interspersed with periods
of recreation.

To better understand a typical day in the life of a Holy
Spirit Adoration Sister, it is first necessary to have some
insight into our daily occupations. The variety of work
within the cloister is really surprising and enables most
talents to be developed and put to good use. As we share
the lot of all humanity, many of our tasks are likewise
similar: housecleaning, washing, ironing, cooking, sewing,
answering doorbells and telephones, caring for our sick
members. However, there is other work which most
people are not aware of since it is more peculiar to our
way of life.

Since our lives revolve around the Eucharist and liturgy there must always be a Sister on hand who cares for preparations involved in the daily celebration of the Eucharist and other liturgical functions. Booklets containing the Vesper service of the day, besides various devotional cards, likewise have to be printed by a Sister for the use of the laity who join us daily for the singing of this part of the Liturgy of the Hours. When we look at the sanctuary and altar of exposition we are reminded that artistic hands took much time and effort to make the lovely floral arrangements. And when we attend liturgical celebrations we know that much practice and time went into the beautiful organ renditions of our Sister-organists and the singing of the Sisters' choir.

Walking down the convent corridor we come to the room where Sisters are busily engaged in using their calligraphy talents to print names on perpetual prayer cards. Requests for these prayer enrollment cards are daily received from people in all walks of life. Adjoining this room is the correspondence department where Sisters help our superior read and answer the many prayer requests received by mail each day. It is no little feat to acknowledge dozens of letters a day but the Sisters take special satisfaction in assuring people of our prayers for their intentions and offering a word of hope and encouragement.

Some of our convents have an altarbread department where hosts for the daily celebration of the Eucharist are baked, cut and packed for mailing to local parishes. This work has always been cherished by our Sisters since we live in such close proximity to the Blessed Sacrament through our lives of perpetual adoration.

Last but not least is our lovely cloister garden. Each of our convents has a large cultivated area within the enclosure for the use and enjoyment of the community. A Sister with a green thumb usually oversees the garden work while some Sisters delight in spending a short time during the day in caring for plants, rooting out weeds, and feeding the inhabitants of our fishpond. The bird-watchers in the community likewise take care that the bird feeders are replenished for their feathered friends.

The subject of gardens seems like a good starting point for a day by day description of our lives, since our garden serves so many purposes. While the garden of each of our various convents has its own peculiar beauty and arrangement, most have an outdoor Way of the Cross and a Lourdes Grotto. Weather permitting, it is refreshing to walk in the midst of the beauty of nature and pray the rosary, make the way of the cross or spend time in reflecting. But even in the midst of all this beauty and tranquillity God will occasionally manifest his sense of humor and permit a bit of distraction. This was the case when our community was presented with a kitten as a gift. The little creature was appointed our official mouse catcher with residence on the lower level of the building, but this kitten loved the garden and whenever possible would sneak outside and wander about. Everything was fine until Sisters came into the garden to pray the rosary. As the Sisters walked down the paths with their rosary beads dangling in front of them, the beads would wave back and forth with the motion of their gait. Evidently this fascinated the little kitten. She would hide behind a bush waiting for an unsuspecting Sister to pass by and then jump out and catch hold of the waving rosary beads. After some gasps from startled Sisters and a few pairs

HOLY SPIRIT ADORATION SISTERS
MOUNT GRACE CHAPEL OF PERPETUAL ADORATION
ST. LOUIS, MISSOURI

THE GARDEN PROVIDES A PEACEFUL ATMOSPHERE FOR PRAYER AND SPIRITUAL REFLECTION.

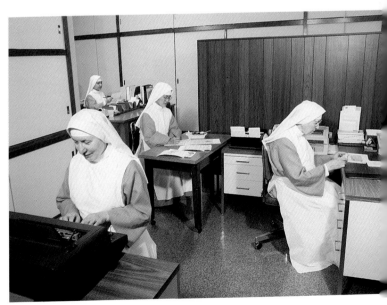

SISTERS ACKNOWLEDGING REQUESTS FOR PRAYERS.

"COME, LET US ADORE HIM!" IT IS OUR PRIVILEGE TO TAKE PART IN PERPETUAL ADORATION OF THE BLESSED SACRAMENT.

ENJOYING A STROLL THROUGH THE GARDEN DURING A RECREATION PERIOD.

SINGING THE PRAISES OF THE LORD DURING THE LITURGY OF THE
HOURS

of broken rosary beads, the kitten was banned from the garden while Sisters were at prayer.

A gazebo in the garden is also a favorite place to sit for spiritual reading or for spending moments of conversation during recreation periods. Some of our convent gardens are equipped with a volleyball/badminton court which is frequented by the younger members of the community who enjoy some extra activity during recreation.

I fondly remember a former superior of our community who had a generous streak when it came to the upkeep of the garden. When questioned about her munificence she replied, "The garden is the only thing the Sisters have within these four walls. It should be nice." There is a bit of good psychology in that statement.

The various tasks and duties along with set times for formal prayer, recreation, silence and all community gatherings, are incorporated into our daily schedule. Being able to adapt to this schedule and allow oneself to be carried along in its flow with a certain amount of serenity is one of the surest signs of a vocation to cloistered-contemplative life. During the course of the day everything we do should be permeated with a spirit of prayer, that is, with an attitude of mind and heart that everything done is for the glory of the Father on behalf of all humanity. When considered in this light the schedule definitely has a sanctifying effect.

Our lives as well as our day centers on the community's celebration of the Eucharist which is preceded by a period of meditation. Times of formal prayer begin in the very early morning. Our first act of the day is one of praise to God and an awareness of his presence as we gather in the chapel to sing part of the Liturgy of the Hours: Morning Prayer. The Liturgy of the Hours, sometimes referred to as the Divine Office, is the official prayer of the Church. It is a spiritually rich collection of psalms expressing praise, thanksgiving and petition, along with scripture passages and readings from the spiritual masters. It is meant to make holy the hours of the day and we return to the chapel at different times to sing the various parts. The final Hour is prayed at the end of the day before retiring for the night. Perhaps the most well-known of these Hours is Evening Prayer, more commonly known as Vespers. Vespers is sung, followed by Benediction of the Blessed Sacrament, in the early evening as members of the clergy and laity join our Sisters for this act of praise.

Throughout the day and night, except when we are gathered together in the chapel for the singing of the Liturgy of the Hours or for the celebration of the Eucharist, one or two Sisters are always kneeling in adoration before the Blessed Sacrament exposed in the monstrance. All time spent in the presence of our Eucharistic Lord is precious but I especially treasure kneeling before him in the quite and darkness of night when all nature is asleep. The atmosphere is one of intimacy and profound peace. This does not mean that it is easy to interrupt the night's rest and spend an hour in prayer, but in spite of any sacrifice entailed, the heart cries out with St. Peter, "Lord, it's good to be here!" (Mk 9:5)

Besides the time given in the schedule for communal or formal prayer, each Sister has an additional hour for personal prayer which includes a period for spiritual reading. Many of the Sisters also use a portion of this hour to pray the rosary and make the way of the cross since these treasured devotions of the Church have a special place in the spiritual heritage of our Congregation.

To provide periods of relaxation during which we can renew our physical and mental energies for the service of the Lord, the Holy Spirit inspired Founders and Foundresses of religious communities to incorporate times of recreation into the schedule. We look forward each evening to our community recreation, which enables us to relax physically and mentally. Besides this community recreation there is an hour of free time in the early afternoon. The Sisters spend this time in a variety of ways: sharing or recreating with each other, working on hobbies and crafts, reading, resting or the like.

Interwoven through our schedule like a golden thread binding all else together, are times of silence, which enable us to listen to the Lord as he reveals himself in our daily lives.

One might ask, "Isn't it monotonous to continually live according to a schedule?" The answer depends on the individual. A person who is always looking for novelty in life will experience a certain amount of monotony in living according to a schedule. Besides, a person who is accustomed to always doing her own thing could fail to see meaning in something she finds distasteful. There is always a certain amount of self-sacrifice in keeping a schedule. However, for someone whole-heartedly intent on pursuing the spiritual life it is an excellent means of discipline in reaching the goal. The schedule imposes a regular pattern of life so that our time each day is accounted for and put to good use. This gives the satisfaction of a full day and a sense of fulfillment. At the same time variety is never wanting. As outside the cloister, so inside the cloister, there are always special happenings, such as a talk from a guest speaker, a visiting missionary with stories about his mission, a special liturgical feastday with a more solemn liturgy and prolonged recreation, that bring change into the day and add spice to life.

There are other elements of time which likewise effect our daily lives, for instance, a special day of the week or the seasons of the liturgical year. Each week I look forward to Sunday as we commemorate the resurrection of Christ and give special thanks to the Blessed Trinity for the graces of creation, redemption and sanctification. Sundays have a spirit all their own as joy and deep peace seem to penetrate every Sister and resound from each nook and corner of the convent.

The liturgical year, which revolves around the mysteries of our Lord's life, takes us through a variety of seasons and is always urging us on to a fuller participation in the life of Christ. There is no life without change. The liturgical year is continually providing us with that change necessary to stimulate and nourish our spiritual life as it takes us from the advent of Christ to the culmination of our redemption in the paschal event.

The season of Advent, which begins the liturgical year, is a time of waiting and expectation. During these weeks we give full attention to our spiritual preparation for the commemoration of Christ's birth on the Feast of Christmas. Among our preparations are the Jesse Tree, a small tree which derives its name from Jesse, the father of King David, and which bears the symbols of salvation history from the fall of our first parents to the coming of Christ. Each evening during the advent season the Sisters gather around this tree to watch, pray and listen as a Sister hangs one of the symbols on the tree and gives an explanation followed by a prayer. This devotion gives us matter for reflection each day as we walk the road of salvation history. The advent wreath, displayed in the sanctuary of our chapel, also has a prominent place in our advent liturgy. Each time we enter the chapel we are reminded by the wreath with its burning candles of the splendor of Christ and his promise to bring us salvation.

As anticipation of the Christmas season mounts, it finds expression not only in the spiritual preparations but also in all the external preparations which seem to overflow from the abundance of the heart. Extra time and effort is put into the practice of the Christmas liturgy which is the highlight of this season as we commemorate the birth of Love Incarnate. The evening recreations are spent in music, song and skits as we celebrate our unity and oneness in Him who is the heart of our community. Amid all the celebration of this feast, a tinge of homesickness is usually felt the first few Christmases in the cloister. A young Sister who was celebrating her fifth Christmas in the convent thought there was something wrong with her that she still experienced a bit of homesickness. She was quite consoled when I told her that it took me about fifteen years before I could honestly say I had no feeling of homesickness during the Christmas season. These feelings, which are such a vivid reminder of our humanity, can serve to unite us more intimately with Him who assumed our human nature, becoming like us in everything except sin. (cf. Heb 4:15)

As the priest marks our forehead with blessed ashes at the beginning of Lent and reminds us that we are dust and shall return to dust, we are confronted anew with our mortality and continual need for conversion. Lent has the atmosphere of a retreat and is perhaps the most grace-filled of all the liturgical seasons as we probe our motives and behavior and seek by means of prayer and positive renunciation to strengthen our inward self for transformation into Jesus Christ.

After reflecting on the paschal mystery in the life of Christ and our own personal life during the final days of Holy Week we give ourselves wholeheartedly to the singing of the alleluias which occur over and over again in the Liturgy of the Hours and the celebration of the Eucharist during the Easter Season. We experience the truth of St. Augustine's words, "We are an Easter people and 'Alleluia' is our song." An atmosphere of joy and triumph pervades our community during these fifty days as we celebrate the victory of Christ, and hence our own victory, over sin and death.

The Feast of Pentecost brings to completion the paschal mystery. By the mission of the Holy Spirit the Good News of Jesus Christ was revealed to the world through the witness of the apostles. Hence during the weeks following Pentecost we are aware of our responsibility as Sisters especially dedicated to the Holy Spirit to contribute to the propagation of the faith and the sanctification of all peoples by our lives of prayer and total dedication. We endeavor to imbibe the spirit of Mother Mary Michael who told us, "For a servant of the Holy Spirit, every day should be a new Pentecost; every breath, 'Come Holy Spirit!'; every deed, 'Send forth your Spirit!';

and every heartbeat, 'Lord Jesus, send us from the Father the Holy Spirit.'"

Time is precious. Whether we adhere to it in the observance of our daily schedule or celebrate it in the progressing of the liturgical seasons, it continually inspires us to live each moment to the best of our ability for "in due time we shall reap our harvest." (Gal 6:9)

4. As I Have Loved You

*"By praying with and for one another, unitedly striving
towards the same goal, and living together as Sisters, we
desire to cultivate persistently the awareness that we are
all one in the Lord in joy and sorrow. Love and kindness,
trustfulness, openness and willingness to forgive should be
characteristic of our community and manifest the presence
of the Spirit of Love in our midst. Herein we have as our
model the Lord, who has commanded us to love one
another as he has loved us."*

– Rule of the Holy Spirit Adoration Sisters

Many years have passed since I walked over the
threshold of our Convent of Divine Love in Philadelphia
and officially began my life as a member of its community.
Little did I realize at the time that I was embarking on an
adventure in communal living that would form me in my
vocation and be one of my greatest supports and challenges. As the cloister door swung open to receive me, I
was filled with awe as I saw two rows of nuns in rose and
white-colored habits: a scene that any T.V. cameraman
would covet! I felt as though I were entering the heavenly
Jerusalem and the saints had gathered to bid me
welcome. As the months and years passed I experienced
community living amid the nitty-gritty of everyday life and
was brought face to face with my own limitations, weaknesses and brokenness (facts which community life has
an excellent way of revealing). The euphoria of the day
of my entrance wore off, but there always remained the
happy reality that it is the presence of our Eucharistic
Lord that creates a heavenly Jerusalem and the women
who accompany me on the pilgrimage of life are indeed

saints in the making.

In praying the Liturgy of the Hours, we frequently sing about how good and how pleasant it is when people live as one. (cf Ps. 133) I have always thought that one of the greatest proofs of the existence of Divine Providence and the authenticity of his call to each Sister is the fact that despite the variety of races and nationalities we represent, the spirit in our community is predominantly one of peace and joy as we strive to attain our common goal. Only Jesus Christ could gather women together, each of whom has a different personality, different attitudes, different values; women who have so little in common except their humanity and the spiritual goals which inspire them, and give them the injunction to live in peace, love and harmony. . . to "live as one." We are made continually aware of the reality that Christ is the "one" we are to be. He is our center, the hub from which we radiate as spokes from a wheel, each moving in a different direction, yet all stemming from the same hub. From that center we receive our strength, direct our efforts, sustain our vision, and draw our inspiration. "In Him we live and move and have our being"–as one.

To delve more deeply into what has just been said, we have to ponder the reality that community is unity in diversity. In Christ we are one. Inspired, motivated and strengthened by his example and words, each of us presses forward to the attainment of our end with a diversity that is the result of our own unique personality, culture and background. God brings together in community people who would have never chosen to live together in other circumstances; yet the diversity that exists among them can make community life beautiful and enriching.

Putting aside our own preferences and inclinations and reaching out in love to one another we build up community and support one another in our mutual endeavor for consummation in God.

God accepts us as we are and where we are in all stages of growth: spiritual, psychological and intellectual.So we, too, must constantly endeavor to do the same for one another. Accepting the little inabilities of others day in and day out requires and fosters patience and forebearance. The everyday necessity of oral communication was a trying experience for our pioneer German Sisters who came to this country to establish our Congregation and also for the first American girls who entered our community. Although our German Sisters studied the English language after their arrival, it took some time before they were fluent enough to communicate intelligibly. This affected the communal prayers and recreation periods, which ended up being a combination of German and English, neither language spoken any too correctly! This situation could be summed up by an incident in which the German superior of the little group telephoned a neighbor to ask a favor. The small son of the family answered and when he heard the accent on the other end of the line, exclaimed, "Hey, Mom, there's a green horn on the phone."

When American candidates entered during this time, they likewise found the language problem somewhat irksome, but decided not to let it discourage them. They set to work learning the German language, and eventually each language group helped the other grow in master of their newly acquired tongue. There are many amusing stories about language blunders made in those days. Often these blunders came at the most inappropriate times, such as, the weekly Chapter of Faults, an exercise in which each Sister mentioned some of her failings and asked pardon of the community. By its very nature it was a solemn exercise in which laughter had little place. But such comments as, "I forgot to forget. . ..... ", or a Sister referring to a spider as a "beast of burden", forced the younger members of the fold to stifle their giggling to the best of their ability. In spite of the many difficulties the Sisters had to overcome during these first years in the U.S., they were animated, strengthened and bound together as one in Christ which enabled them to set their hand to the plow and not look back. (cf Lk 9:62)

Just as community life can bring out the best in a person, the continual interaction with others also makes us aware that we are members of a fallen race and are in continual need of Christ's salvific grace. Weaknesses and limitations that were lost in the sea of our ego and self-esteem because they were never fully challenged, rear their ugly heads. We who always considered ourselves good and kind persons are brought face to face with the truth of our anger, lack of charity, rebelliousness, jealousy, ambition. One of the blessings of community is that we learn to recognize and embrace this dark side of our per-sonality, letting Christ's healing power become active in our lives through reconciliation and forgiveness. When this spirit of reconciliation permeates our relationships with one another and our attitude is one of readiness to forgive gladly and promptly, without bearing grudges, then indeed we experience liberation and are on the way to wholeness.

Communal living offers many advantages. The fact that we are social beings and have an innate need to interact with others is the primary reason why this lifestyle is so satisfying, but it is even more so when its members are motivated by spiritual ideals. The camaraderie that flows from shared living gives us a sense of well-being and belonging, and is a source of strength when difficulties arise. No one is self-sufficient. Time given for verbal sharing is always treasured and helps us to grow in appreciation and understanding of each other. It likewise eases tensions if these should exist. We daily endeavor to intensify our solidarity by living out the words of St. Paul, "If one member suffers, all suffer together; if one member is honored, all rejoice together." (1 Cor 12:26)

Teamwork is one of the essential elements for successful community living. Perhaps teamwork is needed even to a greater extent in a cloistered religious community such as ours, since in this form of lifestyle there are no exterior outlets or distractions, thus intensifying the relations and interactions with each other within the community. Teamwork extends to every facet of our life: communal prayer, work, recreation. However, our "teams" are comprised of unusual combinations: young and old, North and South Americans, Europeans and Asians, highly educated and not-so-highly educated, introverts and extroverts, and a variety of personalities, so that the normal reaction would be to throw up one's hands in exasperation and wonder how such a combination of persons could survive as a team. But survive we do, and perhaps more effectively and happily than those "perfect" combinations matched by computers. Computers are the rage of the age, but the Holy Spirit is infinitely more effective and flawless! Those whom he brings together to form community, diverse as they may be, are united in his love and "eager to maintain the unity of the Spirit in the bond of peace." (Eph 4:3)

In communal prayer we unite our voices in giving praise to God and interceding for his people. Much of our communal prayer, such as the Liturgy of the Hours, is sung at intervals throughout the day. Singing requires even more discipline and teamwork than reciting prayers. Pitch, tone, tempo and articulation have to be given attention and each Sister, according to her God-given talents, cooperates to make it a hymn of praise. The sound of our various accents testifies to the psalm verse we so often sing, "O Praise the Lord, all you nations." (Ps. 117)

Our work comprises a variety of tasks and duties throughout the convent and many of these involve teamwork. A good example was given in an article written about our community. "Dinner is the longest meal. . . . and the clean up is done with an efficiency that might be envied in industry. Each Sister knows what she should do and where she should be. This is the structure they speak of, the smooth flow of prayer and work . . . Since there are no lay Sisters at this convent, the Pink Sisters must fit their manual work – laundry, ironing, baking, cooking, sweeping, gardening, printing, correspondence, bookkeeping – between the times of their most important work, the perpetual adoration of the Blessed Sacrament in the chapel." Although one Sister has the final responsibility for a given work, subsidiary is fostered and encouraged so that each Sister can function with full responsibility within the sphere of her own competence. It is an educational process to observe how Sisters from various cultures can achieve the same end but in different ways. We assimilate this into our own narrow and limited outlook and reap the blessing of becoming a more integrated and whole person. Mention should be made of how enjoyable "integration" can also be at times as, for instance, in our kitchen when often three Sisters of different nationalities work together to prepare the community meals. Each has a distinct way of approaching her task and putting her culinary abilities to use. At the same time the community enjoys an occasional taste of their homeland in German, Filipino and Chinese dishes.

Teamwork also has a place in our daily recreation periods. In our Constitutions we are encouraged to "endeavor to make it (recreation) pleasant for all." Recreation can take many forms: playing games, working on hobbies or puzzles, outdoor sports such as badminton or bicycling. For some it's a time for sitting in the recreation room or walking through the garden as they enjoy friendly conversation and sharing with each other. On certain liturgical feast days and national holidays, special festivities will be planned by groups of Sisters who combine their talents to compose skits and other forms of entertainment. Again teamwork plays a special role in the coordination of these recreational projects which result in anything from a Filipino folk dance to a playlet based on a biblical theme, much to the enjoyment of an appreciative community.

Another important condition for community life is a warm family spirit. When I entered our community I was impressed by the genuine loving concern the Sisters had for one another, manifested in many little ways, but especially in a willingness to always lend a helping hand and in the excellent care given to the sick and elderly. They gave witness to the words of our Founder, Blessed Arnold, "Those Sisters who gladly forget themselves and think of the welfare of others possess the peace and joy of the Holy Spirit who is the God of love." Perhaps one would think that these traits are more characteristic of charity than family spirit, but the two are interrelated. The one cannot exist without the other. A good family spirit is born out of the love and respect members of a community have for each other, and in a willingness to forgive when human weaknesses and limitations surface. Such an atmosphere provides many opportunities for personality and character development.

As we celebrate our oneness in the Lord and his gifts to the community and each member, we also want to avoid the pitfalls of seeking the ideal community. It doesn't exist! Both the community and its members are pilgrims on the way and will experience over and over again the need for conversion and radical change of heart and mind to which the search of the Lord impels us. When and if our expectations of community are not always met, we consider that this is part and parcel of our human life and that a certain loneliness will always remain which can be borne only in a close personal relationship with Christ. The true community will not only provide its members with an atmosphere of fellowship but also an opportunity for moments of solitude by which we intensify our contact with God and are strengthened and fortified for fruitful sharing with each other on all levels.

As Holy Spirit Adoration Sisters the Blessed Sacrament is the heart and center of our communal life. In the Eucharist, Jesus is living bread for the nourishment of us all, and so we must be bread for each other. A familiar saying of Mother Mary Michael was, "In the light of the Eucharistic Sun, let us joyfully serve the Lord." As we bask in the rays of the Eucharistic Christ, we imbibe his life-giving Spirit and project to each other the truth of the words of the psalmist, "How good and pleasant it is when people live as one."

5. In His Spirit

"At the core of Blessed Arnold's spirituality lies the mystery of the Blessed Trinity. He consecrated his life to glorifying the triune God. . . Like him, we strive to glorify the triune God in everything and endeavor to live, pray, work and suffer under his loving gaze. With Father Arnold we are convinced that by our hidden life of prayer and sacrifice we serve the Church in its missionary task and alleviate the needs of mankind."

— Rule of the Holy Spirit Adoration Sisters

About a week after my entrance into our community, I was enjoying a recreation period with the novitiate group when a novice turned to me and asked, "What attracted you to our Congregation?" I was a little bewildered since it was simply the cloistered-contemplative lifestyle that attracted me and an inner conviction that this was the community for me. As time passed I, too, began asking that same question of other Sisters and was always a little fascinated at the answers received. Although the answers differed, it is evident that the Sisters were drawn by different aspects of the spirituality with which the Holy Spirit endowed our Congregation through the instrumentality and charism of our Founder, Blessed Arnold.

Many of our Sisters were attracted by our apostolate of perpetual adoration of the Blessed Sacrament, others by our dedication and devotion to the Holy Spirit, or the Congregation's aim of prayer and sacrifice for priests. One Sister knew she had to enter a community that had the daily singing of the Liturgy of the Hours because she had become acquainted with this form of prayer while still at home and it had become such a vital part of her prayer-life.

These main features of the spirituality of our Congregation are intertwined with less known factors which, as a whole, vitalize and bear fruit for the spiritual life and development of our Congregation and its members, thereby, enabling us to live daily in His Spirit. To better understand our spirituality I would like to begin this explanation at the source of all spirituality, the holy triune God.

Our spirituality is, first and foremost, rooted in the **Blessed Trinity.** This is our legacy from Blessed Arnold who made the triune God the foundation not only of his prayer life and spirituality, but of his every breath and heartbeat as is indicated in the little prayer he often said, "Take every breath and every beat of my heart as an act of love and veneration of thee, O holy and triune God." He centered everything on the three Divine Persons: Father, Son and Holy Spirit, and wished the members of the three religious Congregations he established to do the same. He bequeathed to us the so-called Quarter-hour Prayer which is a repeated renewal every quarter of an hour of faith, hope and love, together with petitions for oneness in Christ and for the Holy Spirit, so that we might be conscious of the triune God's presence over and over again during the day. In all our convents a clock chimes every quarter of an hour to remind us of this prayerful practice. He chose as motto of our Congregation the maxim, "May the holy triune God live in our hearts and in every heart."

From our rootedness in the Blessed Trinity there blossoms the two basic devotions of our spirituality, each of

45

which is mentioned in the title of our Congregation: Holy
Spirit Adoration Sisters. The first, devotion to the **Holy
Spirit** to whom we are especially consecrated, is the hall-
mark of our community. Our Rule states: "As in the life of
our Founder and in accord with his wish, the Holy Spirit
and his saving work receive a prominent place in our life
of faith and in our piety. In the Holy Spirit, we adore the
Father and acknowledge Jesus as our Lord; we allow
ourselves to be drawn into the mystery of the triune God
and his saving plan. We glorify the Holy Spirit especially
in our readiness to let ourselves be led by his love and
in remaining receptive and docile to his inspirations."

Blessed Arnold received this spiritual legacy from his
parental home. His father, Gerard Janssen, attended
Mass every Monday in honor of the Holy Spirit and often
spoke to his children with great enthusiasm about the
blessings and graces that flow from devotion to the third
Person of the Blessed Trinity. It is no wonder that Blessed
Arnold dedicated the two Sisterhoods he founded to the
Holy Spirit.

In keeping with the wish of our Founder, our religious
habit with its rose-colored garment is a distinctive sign of
our consecration to the Holy Spirit. From the earliest days
of our Congregation's existence, this Pentecostal color of
our habit influenced people to call us, "The Pink Sisters."
This nickname has followed us to the four continents
where we have foundations, and even beyond. The cruci-
fix we receive at first profession of vows as well as the
ring which we receive at perpetual profession, bear a
symbol of the Holy Spirit.

The second basic devotion of our spirituality is the
Blessed Sacrament. Our relationship to the Eucharist is

manifested in adoration which is our life task. According to the circumstances of each of our convents, we maintain this adoration day and night before the exposed Blessed Sacrament. The Eucharist imparts to us that love which must animate us in our apostolate of prayer and sacrifice. It is the heart of our community and the visible efficacious sign of our union with God and with one another.

Pope John XXIII said, "The cloistered Sister adoring before the Tabernacle is the most effective representative of mankind." As we kneel before the Eucharistic Christ in adoration, he sees in us all humanity whom we represent and to whom we are bound through him who is Lord and Savior of all. We, in turn, see present in the Host the Body of Christ, especially the afflicted and needy members, the ones whom Jesus called the "least of my brothers."

In our efforts to promote the glorification of the Blessed Sacrament and to provide all people with an opportunity to deepen their personal relationship with Christ, we consider it part of our apostolate to have our chapels of perpetual adoration open daily to the public. Members of the laity, as well as priests and religious, participate daily in the Eucharistic celebration and in sung Vespers.

In 1958, under the direction of the late Joseph Cardinal Ritter, Archbishop of St. Louis, Rev. Joseph A. McNicholas, a parish priest of St. Louis, who was later appointed bishop of Springfield, IL, organized and initiated the Legion of One Thousand Men at Mount Grace Chapel. The condition of membership was to unite with our Sisters in their adoration before the Blessed Sacrament by making at least one visit a week. This endeavor was a grand success with weekly visits by Legion men alone totaling over 2,500 within a short time.

The idea of the Legion was introduced into our other chapels throughout the world and the result has been a variety of different types of organizations, such as The Womens' Adorers League, The King's Men, The Eucharistic League Members, and Ladies of the Eucharist, in which people join our Sisters in adoration before the Blessed Sacrament, whether for a short visit or a longer period of time.

If Jesus' life is one of surrender and dedication "for the life of the world," (Jn 6:51) then our life also, spent in the presence of the Eucharistic Lord and under the guidance of the Holy Spirit, must become more and more a life of selfless surrender to the Father and unconditional dedication for the salvation of humankind. From these attributes of selfless surrender and unconditional dedication comes another dimension of our spirituality: **Readiness for Service.** Readiness to serve does not mean to serve according to one's own ideas, but according to the need of the other. This readiness demands self-renunciation and self-emptying. Within our religious community there has to be a readiness to work where our service is needed in order to help the community attain its aims and fulfill its mission. This work can be anything from mopping up a floor to answering the telephone, anywhere from St. Louis, Missouri to Baguio City in the Philippine Islands.

In our relationship to all humanity, this readiness for service is especially manifest in **intercessory prayer.** Our Rule states, "Open to the intentions and concerns of the Church as well as to the needs of all, we intercede before God in their behalf. . . Every distress and hardship in the world should find a vigorous response in our prayer."

We are especially mindful of our Lord's exhortation: "Ask the Lord of the harvest to send workers to his harvest," and respond with **prayer and sacrifice for priests,** a special obligation given us by Bl. Arnold. Conscious that the evangilization of the world cannot be realized without good priests who, in the spirit of Jesus, the eternal high priest, will lead the people of God, our intercession is offered by day and night first and foremost for those engaged in the work of proclaiming the good news. During every hour of nocturnal adoration, the Sisters intercede for priests, living and deceased, by either praying the Marian rosary or another form of prayer.

No matter for whom our prayers are specifically offered, our life of prayer as a whole is for the honor and glory of the triune God and the salvation of all people. Contemplation and intercession are not mutually exclusive; they belong together. They are intertwined in a simple wordless gesture. If our life is totally dedicated to God, it is a continuous intercession, even when we are not expressly formulating intercessory prayers. In contemplation we turn first to God and his love; from his love we arrive at the needs of mankind. In intercession we turn first to mankind and its needs, and arrive at God who can alleviate every need.

Another prominent feature of a Holy Spirit Adoration Sister is her vocation to participate in the Church's **Missionary Role.** Having previously founded the missionary Society of the Divine Word (S.V.D.) and the Holy Spirit Missionary Sisters (S.Sp.S.), it was our Founder's dream that we support and complement their activity. Wherever we are our prayer sustains the missionary activity of the Church in the whole world. Nevertheless, we also endeavor to establish as many chapels of perpetual adoration as possible in territories where the knowledge and love of Jesus Christ is not yet firmly rooted. Therefore, you will find our chapels of perpetual adoration in a metropolis such as Berlin, Manila or Philadelphia and, likewise, our Sisters can be found endeavoring to build up the body of Christ by the service of their witness and example rendered in our contemplative life in remote districts of India and Brazil.

Perhaps one of the most distinctive signs of the missionary dimension of our community lies within our form of government. Unlike most other cloistered-contemplative Orders, our individual monasteries are not autonomous and self-governing. Instead we have a central form of government headed by our superior general and her two councillors. Each of these three Sisters are from a different continent and represent our monasteries in Europe, America and Asia. This form of government enables our convents worldwide to aid each other, both in regard to personnel and finances.

Binding all the features of our spirituality together in one harmonious act of worship is our total commitment to the triune God by our **vows**. Impelled by the love poured into our hearts by the Holy Spirit, we bind ourselves by vows to consecrated chastity, evangelical poverty and apostolic obedience. Thus we attain great stability and freedom to love God with undivided heart and to devote ourselves entirely to our vocational tasks.

A commentary on the spirituality of the Holy Spirit Adoration Sisters would be incomplete without mention of Mary, the Mother of the Lord and Immaculate Spouse of the Holy Spirit. We look to her as a model of faithful, loving attentiveness to God's word. She kept the word in her Immaculate Heart, followed it, and thus dedicated herself entirely to the mystery of redemption. It is she who leads us to union with God and fruitful service to the Church and all peoples.

The Feast of Mary's Immaculate Conception, December 8, is the foundation day of our Congregation. It was on this day in 1896 that Bl. Arnold officially established our community and entrusted its spiritual and temporal welfare to the motherly solicitude of the Virgin Mary. With her we sing of the great things God has done and will continue to do for us as we let ourselves be led ever deeper into the inestimable riches of the spirituality bequeathed to us by Blessed Arnold Janssen.

6. Springs of Life

"By this way of life we witness to the basic truth that God is the true center of being and the goal of history and that he alone can satisfy the human heart."

– Rule of the Holy Spirit Adoration Sisters

A favorite psalm of contemplative persons is Psalm 42: "As the deer thirsts for running waters, so my soul thirsts for you, my God." Its theme of the soul longing for God's presence is likewise the theme of contemplative life. This thirst for God urges us each day to seek ways and means to find him ever more intensely until we are satiated with everlasting possession of him. The Rule and Constitutions of our Congregation provide us with some of these ways and means which, at the same time, help form us as Holy Spirit Adoration Sisters.

Among these is the enclosure which characterizes our lifestyle as cloistered-contemplative religious women. The enclosure is usually the biggest stumbling block to understanding the value of our way of life and our particular service to the world. We are certainly aware that God can be found everywhere and anywhere and that prayer is not confined within four walls. But it is not the visible signs of enclosure, such as walls and grilles, that are important in themselves but rather the seclusion they provide. Our contemplative life requires seclusion of which our enclosure is the sign and form. Jesus himself reiterates the importance of solitude for the nurturing of our spiritual energies, when he said, "Come away by yourselves to a lonely place." (Mk 6:31) Our enclosure is not a negative withdrawal, but a place set apart in which we can continually seek God, experience aloneness with him and simply **be** for the glory of the Father.

There have always been and will always be some individuals who feel drawn to intimacy with God which the seclusion of enclosure makes possible. There is a desire to intensify within themselves the vocation of every baptized soul which St. Paul speaks of when he said, "For you have died and your life is hidden with Christ in God." (Col 3:3).

The effects of the enclosure within my life began even prior to my entrance. The inner urge that continually drew me to a cloistered-contemplative life was God's gift of vocation at work. However, to make the final decision to follow this call was not easy. There was an inner conflict: following my dream, versus, the pain of physical separation from loved ones and from certain legitimate pleasures of life. When the news about my upcoming entrance spread among friends and acquaintances, it caused different reactions. There were those who valued contemplative life and thought my decision was wonderful. Then there was the group who thought I was crazy to be "throwing away my life" and, lastly, the few who thought I was being inconsiderate of my twice-widowed mother. Fortunately, my mother was supportive of my vocation and had the faith to realize that physical separation is replaced by a union of spirits intensified by God's love and nurtured by daily prayer. For the first time in my life I experienced the sting of prejudice: to have a neighbor snub me and not acknowledge my presence, and a good friend cross the street in order to avoid passing me by. And yet, the experience was a good one. It made me re-evaluate my own spiritual values, especially the purpose and value of enclosure and vowed commitment to God.

Occasionally people will be taken aback when they
enter our chapel or convent reception room for the first
time and see the grille, sign and symbol of our enclosure.
And yet, the grille is rich in meaning and symbolism.
Some years ago a priest jotted down his musings on the
grille which he defined "as a point of encounter between
two existential solitudes in search of the totally Other."
The following are his thoughts:

- "A wall to keep you in, or a barrier to keep me out
  Or none such, but. . . point of encounter?
- In between you and me, a space neither can enter.
  A special most sacred space. . . point of encounter.
- Hindrance? Encumbrance?
  Or entrance into the inside of 'deep down things'?
- The Grille - real - speaks of you and me.
  Beyond utterance, the unutterable;
  Beyond entrance, the impenetrable;
  Hidden presence, deep inside;
  Veiled vastness, open wide;
  Beyond touch, the intangible;
  Beyond reach, the unreachable;
  The mystery of you and me,
  Inexpressible, incommunicable - we.
  The Grille - real - speaks of you and me.
- In its presence we are. . .
  filled with a sense of mystery,
  faced with a kind of restless dissatisfaction,
  not in life's emptiness
  but in its fullness.
  Longing, unsatisfied,
  We eat yet hunger -
  Drink yet thirst. . . only to
  Behold! Adore! the Lord.

And when you really come down to it and put aside philosophical meanderings, wanderings, and wonderings, the Grille tells us:

'O time-bound-limited creature,
You can't have it all on this side of life's fence.'"

Children are usually the most mystified by the grille. This was evident when one of our novices received a visit from her family shortly after the birth of another child. Sister's younger brothers and sisters were very excited that she was gong to see her new little brother for the first time and they wanted her to hold him. They were not too satisfied with the explanation Sister Mary Ann gave about holding little Jimmy in her heart instead of her arms. The moment Sister became absorbed in conversation with her parents, they swooped up the baby, put it in the turnstile and swung the turnstile around thereby depositing little Jimmy in the enclosure, much to the consternation and amusement of Sister and her parents.

It is a consolation that even the saints keenly felt the sacrifice of leaving family and loved ones, as St. Therese of Lisieux wrote in her autobiography when she described her farewell to her father and family at the time of her entrance into Carmel. She comments on the pain of that parting and adds that only those who have had this experience know the suffering entailed. How true! But at the same time they alone know the deep joy and profundity of stepping into the enclosure and experiencing the words of the Psalmist, "How lovely is your dwelling place, Lord God of hosts. . . For a day in your courts is better than a thousand elsewhere." (Ps. 84)

For me the expression "God alone" is synonymous with the cloister. On the other hand it seems paradoxical that my desire to help all peoples led me to a lifestyle that limits my physical contact with others and prevents me from actively being of service to them. And yet it is this very desire to touch as many souls as possible that led me to the enclosure where a spirit of prayer envelops all that we are and do, and reaches far beyond the confines of the grille to touch the Heart of Christ on behalf of all humanity.

The enclosure is one of the best schools available for humanitarian and sacred studies! It teaches us explicitly what it means to be gradually transformed into the likeness of Christ thus preparing us for final consummation in the Father. At the same time it is amazing how much one learns when daily confronted with one's self, others, situations and circumstances without even the alleviation of being able to take a walk down the street! Anyone who accuses cloistered nuns of running away from life has little knowledge or understanding of cloistered life. A person who embarks on a deep spiritual life must be prepared to come face to face with the God of light and truth. In the cloister there are no outside distractions, no external activities or entertainments, no radio or T.V. to lessen the intensity of this confrontation but there is always and only God, me, and the reality. It is a treasured grace to take advantage of these opportunities and allow the light of the Holy Spirit to fill us so that the truth will be recognized and we can experience the inner freedom which Jesus speaks of when he says, "and the truth will set you free." (Jn 8:32) Then we possess that deep peace "which the world cannot give" and which is synonymous with truth.

Spiritual benefits of the enclosure would be non-exis-
tent without silence. Pope Paul VI said, "The search for
intimacy with God involves the truly vital need of a silence
embracing the whole being." Exterior silence is but a har-
binger of inner silence which disposes the heart and
mind to absorb the presence of the living God. It is in
this silence and calm that God usually reveals himself.
Although there are likewise times for cheerful conversation and mutual sharing in our daily life, we endeavor to
create an atmosphere of silence out of love and respect
for each other in our spiritual journey together.

Some persons regard silence as something morbid
and depressing, but they have never experienced silence
in a cloister. One of my first impressions during the days
after my entrance was that silence speaks louder than
words. Never before had I seen so many smiling faces or
experienced such merriment over the small happenings of
life! How it cheered my heart to receive a big smile from
every Sister I passed in the corridor, smiles that made me
feel I belonged and was lovingly accepted as a "family"
member. Not a word was every spoken at these encoun-
ters but words were not necessary. The smiles told me
that there was deep inner joy in the heart of each Sister
as a result of the divine intimacy she daily nurtured
through silence.

Just as silence has an important role in our contemplative life, so also our daily recreation period. Recreation
means to re-create, and we endeavor with each recreation period to re-create and re-vitalize that harmony
existing between body, soul and spirit so that our hidden
lives of prayer and sacrifice may become every more
enriching and fruitful. The value of silence during the day

is experienced in recreation. Little stories and happenings of the day waiting to be shared with each other during recreation, spill over into lively and animated conversation interspersed with billows of laughter. When some of our elderly Sisters begin losing their hearing in the aging process and forget the sounds of our lively exchanges during recreation, they are startled back to awareness when they get a hearing aid. This was evident in our Sister Mary Raphaela who enthusiastically came to recreation for the first time with her new hearing aid and stood flabbergasted at the recreation room doorway as she exclaimed, "It sounds like a menagerie!"

A continual source of living water to which we have recourse each day for spiritual strength, refreshment and support is the Liturgy of the Hours. When we gather together as a community at intervals during the day, we unite ourselves with Christ and the whole Church to sing this hymn of praise to the Father. As we enter into this dialogue with God our faith, hope and love find abundant nourishment thus enabling the dialogue to continue throughout all the hours of the day.

The process of continual formation is a spring of life that is always flowing and never runs dry in our religious life. After the definitive periods of formation during the postulancy, novitiate and time of temporary profession in which each Sister participates, formation continues after perpetual profession of vows and takes various forms. One of the Constitutions in our Holy Rule explains it well, "The process of formation does not terminate with perpetual profession. Throughout our lives we should earnestly endeavor to perfect our spiritual, doctrinal, and practical development. Therefore we gladly take advantage of all that is offered us for our growth and try to make it our own."

One of the first steps to our ongoing formation is the availability of suitable periodicals and books. Our library has a wide selection of books on the spiritual life besides various topics which are conducive to our formation as well-integrated religious women. Competent persons are periodically engaged to give talks on topics that will benefit our cloistered-contemplative vocation, such as the spiritual life, the vows, prayer, Church history, the Fathers of the Church, and psychology which helps promote sound communal living.

"Jesus stood up and proclaimed, 'If any one thirsts let him come to me and drink.'" (Jn 7:37) In living our vocation as Holy Spirit Adoration Sisters, we have daily recourse to this fountain of life-giving water through the spirituality and charisms of our Congregation. Our united efforts and loyal perseverance give testimony to the power of Christ and of the Holy Spirit in our lives as we journey together to the attainment of our goal and the realization of our shared dream.

Epilogue

As time passes our dream becomes ever more a reality as the reign of God becomes increasingly present within us as individuals and as a community, and through the growth and expansion of our Congregation. Every day echoes with the incessant call of God beckoning us on to a more radical giving of self. In responding to this call, we experience his activity within our community and within ourselves as we, "beholding the glory of the Lord, are being changed into his likeness from one degree of glory to another." (2 Cor. 3:18)

The growth of our Congregation includes eighteen chapels of perpetual adoration established throughout the world. From these sanctuaries of prayer God's graces flow, touching the lives of people of every race and creed, that all may experience the salvation of Christ and be united in him and with him for the glory of the Father.

Our Rule tells us, "When in death Christ calls us home to behold the triune God face to face, we are finally taken up into the love which unites Father and Son in the Holy Spirit and continue in the light of eternal glory the adoration we began in this life in the darkness of faith." (Article 420)

A dream come true!